How Animals Behave

Animal Navigators

Jeremy Cherfas

Lerner Publications Company
Minneapolis

Contents

Introduction

Have you ever been so lost that you didn't know which way to go? I have. I was in a strange city with cars screeching past me as I struggled with a map. I had to find out where I was, where I wanted to be, and how to get there. I had to navigate.

Navigation is the science of finding your way around. You might be on a short trip—figuring out how to get home after the first day at a new school. Or you could be taking a longer journey—from your home to the ocean or the mountains for a vacation. Humans use street signs, landmarks, maps, compasses, and even computers to find their way through unfamiliar territory.

Animals, too, are excellent navigators. But animals navigate without maps or street signs. Some animals seem to have a built-in sense of direction. They know where to go without having to learn their way. Others learn their way by trial and error. Some follow signposts on the land and in the sea and the sky. Some animals make regular long journeys. The Arctic tern, for instance, flies almost all the way from the South Pole to the North Pole to breed each year. Other animals go on shorter journeys. The limpet, a small sea mollusk, creeps from its shelter on a rock to feed several feet away. No matter how long the journey, all animals need to navigate.

An Arctic tern in flight. Every year, these birds fly over 6,600 miles (11,000 km) from the Antarctic to their Arctic breeding grounds.

A huge flock of migrating snow geese and Canada geese

1 / Movement and Migration

Most scientists distinguish between animal migration and other kinds of movement. Migration is a long journey, back and forth. It is usually made regularly, such as every year. Swallows migrate. They spend half the year breeding in Europe or North America and then migrate to Africa or South America where they spend the rest of the year feeding. Other animal movement is not always between fixed places and does not happen so regularly. A water vole is a rodent that often leaves the safety of its nest in a burrow and wanders around looking for food or a mate. The vole does not travel at one particular time of the year. The water vole moves, but it does not migrate.

Why Migrate?

You may wonder why an animal needs to migrate from one place to another. If an area is a good home, why not stay there? Animals migrate because a home may be good at some times but not at others. Many birds breed in one place and spend the rest of the year somewhere else. Usually the breeding area has plenty of food, but only for a short while.

This bald eagle has caught a migrating salmon.

In winter months, the Arctic tundra freezes over and cannot support life. Caribou and other animals migrate south in herds as winter approaches. Caribou antlers can be seen in the foreground.

The frozen **tundras** in Arctic lands are such places. Most of the year, tundra lands are cold and barren. But in the spring, tundras come to life with animals and swarms of insects. Flocks of birds arrive in the tundras to breed and to feed on the small insects. Come winter, however, the birds have to find somewhere warmer that has more food. So off they fly.

Learning about Migration

Ancient peoples knew that animals came and went with the seasons. The Indians of the Pacific Coast of North America gathered by rivers each spring to catch salmon that were swimming upstream to mate. Brown bears and bald eagles would join the Indians. All would feast on the migrating fish.

The Indians made up myths and stories to explain nature's bounty. Ancient peoples in all parts of the world noticed that animals vanished at some times of the year, and they too tried to explain it.

In Alaska, a brown bear tries to catch a leaping salmon as the fish migrates upstream to breed.

The Ancient World

Aristotle, the Greek philosopher who lived between 384 and 322 B.C., wrote about migration in one of his books. He knew that some animals went south in the winter and returned in the spring. He noticed that in a migrating flock of pelicans, each bird would take a turn flying at the front. He also discovered that when birds were about to migrate they would grow fatter—the fat giving them an extra fuel supply. All this is true, but Aristotle made one mistake that was not corrected until the 18th century. He thought that some birds, most notably swallows, did not migrate at all but simply **hibernated** through the winter. Aristotle claimed that in winter you could sometimes find birds asleep in holes. In fact, the birds he saw were probably dead. But Aristotle's idea that swallows hibernate lasted a long time. Some people even thought that the birds plunged into the water and buried themselves in the mud at the bottom of streams.

A flock of white pelicans traveling from northern Europe flies over Israel. These large birds fish together and fly in formation.

Swallows live in the Northern Hemisphere in the summer. As winter approaches, the birds migrate south to warmer places such as Central America, North Africa, and northern Australia.

Part of the problem for people trying to study migration in earlier times was that travel was far more difficult for people than it was for birds. There was no way to follow the birds and see where they went. The breakthrough came when someone decided to mark a bird by putting a ring around its leg.

Banding Birds

One of the first people to ring, or band, a bird was a nobleman who lived over 200 years ago. The nobleman banded a swallow that had made its nest in a chateau in France. He discovered that the banded bird returned to the same nest three years in a row. Of course, the band did not tell the man where the bird went when it was not at the chateau.

Banding (above) helps scientists to learn about bird migration. Banding is painless for the bird, and the bands are so light that they do not interfere with flight. On the left is a bird-banding station in Israel. Radar is also used to study bird migration.

In 1899 a scientist in Denmark made the first aluminum bands for birds. Similar bands are still used. These bands are very light, they won't rust, and they last a long time. Each band is stamped with a number and the address of the person who banded the bird. If you find a bird with a band, contact the owner with the date and the bird's location. This will help scientists learn how long birds live, where they go, and how fast they travel.

In Britain about half a million birds are banded each year. Birds ringed in Britain have appeared in Australia, South America, and even on the eastern coast of the Soviet Union. Conversely, banded birds from all over the world have turned up in Britain. Without these bands, we would know far less about bird migration.

Studying Animal Movements

Banding is one method that lets us follow bird migrations. There are similar tags for other kinds of animals—even fish. There are many other techniques that help scientists study bird migration. **Radar** operators peering at their radar screens often see flocks of birds passing through the sky. With radar, scientists can measure the speed and direction in which the birds are traveling and can sometimes identify the **species** and size of the flock.

A gharial, a relative of the crocodile, is fitted with a radio transmitter and released in Nepal.

Some scientists use an activity cage to record the direction an animal wants to travel. One of the simplest activity cages is made of an inked pad placed at the bottom of a cone of paper. A bird that has been captured during its migration will try to climb out of the cone in the direction that it normally migrates. The bird will leave inky footprints that show which direction it wants to go. A more high-tech activity cage might have perches connected to a computer that records the bird's movements.

Some scientists have used airplanes to follow birds and butterflies. Others have attached radio transmitters to animals and tracked their migration via satellites that pick up the radio signals high above the Earth. Scientists have now mapped out the exact journeys of whales, seals, and even albatrosses, and we are finally beginning to understand how animals migrate. Of all the animals that migrate, we know most about birds.

Above: tracking condors by radio signals in California. Below: a Canada goose fitted with a lightweight radio transmitter as well as a band.

9

2 / Navigating in the Air: Birds

The blackpoll warbler is a little bird that spends its summers in New England in the northeastern United States. As winter approaches, the birds go on a feeding binge, doubling their weight in just two weeks. The extra fat is needed to power four or five days of nonstop flying. One evening, when there is a wind from the northwest, the birds take off over the Atlantic Ocean. They pass over Bermuda and the Caribbean Sea. Finally they land in Brazil in South America, 2,400 miles (4,000 kilometers) away. While New England is blanketed with snow, the birds are feasting on tropical insects in Brazil. In the spring, they turn around and fly back north, taking a slightly different route.

Strong wings and tail feathers help the blackpoll warbler make its remarkable long-distance flight, shown on the map below.

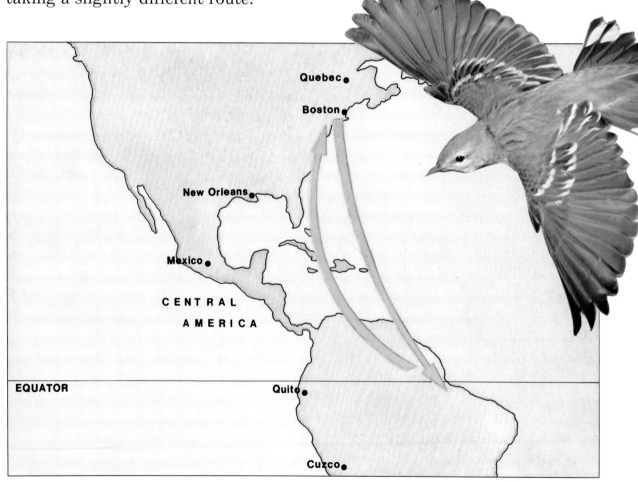

Quebec

Boston

New Orleans

Mexico

CENTRAL AMERICA

EQUATOR

Quito

Cuzco

The 4,800-mile (8,000-km) round trip of the black-poll warbler is just one example of the fantastic travels of many birds. The Arctic tern travels 6,600 miles (11,000 km) from Antarctica to the Arctic. Some birds are precision navigators. The Laysan albatross flies over and around the vast Pacific Ocean for two or three years. Then, when it is time to breed, the bird find its way home to Midway Island, its breeding ground, a target of only 2 square miles (5 square km).

A young Laysan albatross lands at Midway Island in the Pacific Ocean.

How Do Birds Navigate?

It seems very mysterious that birds should be able to find their way around so accurately without any visible map or compass. How do they know where they are? How do they know they are flying in the right direction? Scientists have watched thousands of birds of many different species to find the answers.

Birds that migrate at night, like the European robin, can navigate by the stars. But instead of using a single star, the way people have used the North Star for guidance, the robins use the whole pattern of stars that can be seen around the North Pole. Young robins raised in a planetarium will use the stars in the planetarium as their compass.

It is difficult for scientists to study bird migration because most birds migrate only twice a year. So scientists have turned to a bird that navigates "to order"—the homing pigeon.

Homing Pigeons

Homing pigeons are quite extraordinary navigators. They can be taken from their home loft, put into baskets, and moved hundreds of miles away, and when the baskets are opened, the pigeons will rush out and head straight home. It is no wonder biologists have tried to solve the mysteries of migration by studying homing pigeons.

Scientists have found that these birds use many methods to find their way home. If they are only a few miles away, they simply check the familiar landmarks, which they know from previous flights. Farther from home, the pigeons steer by the sun.

The sun rises in the east and sets in the west. To fly east all day, a bird must fly toward the sun in the morning and away from the sun in the afternoon. Animals can use the sun as a compass to help them stay on course—as long as they know the time of day.

But what do they do at noon? At certain times of the year, the sun passes directly overhead at noon. During the rest of the year, however, the sun passes over in the south or the north at noon. How far the sun travels from the horizon depends upon where you are on Earth when you observe the sun. When pigeons navigate, they rely on knowing where the

A pigeon breeder with his racing pigeon. Before the invention of the telegraph, pigeons were used to carry messages. Now people race pigeons over various distances, sometimes as much as 600 miles (1,000 km).

A group of white pigeons at the entrance to their loft

When these racing pigeons are released from their transporter, they will fly right to their home loft.

sun should stand in the sky at all times of the day.

Animal navigators can be fooled into thinking a noontime sun in the south is really a morning sun low in the east. Scientists have shifted pigeons' internal clocks. They held the birds for several days in a room where the lights were turned on and off six hours earlier than sunrise or sunset. When the pigeons were released in the morning, they read the easterly sun as a midday sun standing in the south. They therefore thought north was roughly opposite the sun and they flew in that direction. Since the sun was really in the east, they flew in a westerly direction.

Pigeons use other navigational instruments besides the sun. When the sky is overcast and the sun is invisible, they are still able to navigate. Scientists think that some birds have a built-in magnetic compass. The Earth has a stronger magnetic pull at the North and South poles. Some scientists believe that pigeons can sense this magnetic pull and use it to stay on course.

Birds will also follows sounds, such as the crashing of waves on a beach, and will use their sense of smell to find their destination. Of course, birds use their eyes to find familiar landmarks. When homing pigeons are unable to see clearly, they can head in the right direction, but they have trouble finding their home precisely.

Learning and Instinct

Nobody knows for certain how birds learn to find their way using the sun or stars as guides. Nor do we know exactly how their magnetic sense works. Despite extensive research, many things about bird navigation remain a mystery.

There is also a puzzle surrounding those birds that migrate from their breeding grounds. How do the young birds, those that have never made the journey before, know where to go to find their wintering areas? Some, like the Bewick's swans that fly from Siberia to England, travel with their parents and learn the route that way. But others, such as cuckoos, never see their parents. They are raised by other birds that don't migrate with them. Yet cuckoos still manage to find their way from Europe to Africa. This kind of unlearned behavior is called **instinct**.

Birds feeding at the Wildfowl Trust in Welney, England. The birds in the foreground are Bewick's swans. They summer in the tundras in the northern Soviet Union and migrate to warmer lands, including England and northern Europe, in October.

Some starlings migrate. These starlings assemble on an English building before flying off together. They know just how far apart they need to perch so they do not hit one another's wings when they take off.

Many birds navigate by a combination of learning and instinct.

Some starlings, for example, nest near the Baltic Sea in northern Europe. In autumn, they fly southwest to the Netherlands and then across the North Sea to England. A Dutch scientist once caught some starlings, put bands on them, and took them to Switzerland. First he released the young starlings. When they had vanished, the scientist released the adults. In that way, the young birds were not able to follow the adults.

The adults ended up in northern France, and some even made it to England. Even though the scientist had moved them, they navigated properly, changing their course to end up in the right place. But the young birds turned up in Spain and the south of France. They had simply flown on in the same direction they were headed earlier. This experiment shows that the birds had an instinctive sense for which way to go. But they could also learn to change their direction when they were put off course.

This barnacle goose has just arrived at its tundra breeding ground in northern Canada. People in ancient times believed that these birds hatched from barnacles in the sea.

3 / Navigating in the Air: Bees

When a worker bee, called a **scout**, flies out in search of food, it usually meanders along, twisting and turning. But after finding food, it makes a "beeline" straight back to the hive, knowing exactly where the hive is. Like the homing pigeon, the bee navigates by using the sun as a compass.

Using the Sun

A simple experiment proves that bees use the sun for navigation. Scientists have found that if you set out sugar water near a beehive, say due east, you can train the bees to feed there. Then if you shut the bees in their hive for a few days and, just as with the pigeons, change the pattern of light and darkness, you can fool the bees into thinking that it is dawn when it is really noon.

When you let the bees out of the hive to feed at noon, they will think it is dawn and fly straight toward the sun. The bees think the sun is due east and this is where they have learned their food is. But since it is really noon, the sun is not in the east. The bees will end up in the wrong place.

Bees have many devices that enable them to navigate so well. The bee's antennae provide it with the senses of smell and touch. The bee also has a large compound eye on each side of its head. The compound eyes enable bees to see patterns of polarized light in the sky.

Two worker honeybees approach a flower in their search for nectar. The antennae of the bee on the right point toward the flower.

The sun, of course, is not always visible. But bees can still navigate under cloudy skies because they can detect other clues. They can see **polarized light** that humans cannot see. Polarized light creates patterns in the sky, and bees use these patterns to find their course in relation to the sun. It is possible that bees can also detect the Earth's magnetic field just as birds do.

How Bees Give Directions

When a scout gets back to the beehive, it dances on the honeycomb. The scout's dance actually tells the other bees where the food is. The scout runs along the comb in a figure-eight pattern, waggling from side to side. The other workers follow the dance and soon set off in search of the food. They find it so quickly that they must have been given precise directions. But how?

Worker bees at the entrance to their hive. They come and go busily in their hunt for pollen and nectar. Worker bees have other jobs besides hunting for food. They must also fan their wings near the hive entrance to keep the hive cool.

The Dance of the Bees

Karl von Frisch, an Austrian scientist, discovered how the scout's dance tells the other worker bees where to go to find food. Von Frisch marked each bee that arrived at a feeding station with a spot of paint. Back at the hive, he watched the marked bee dance. Gradually von Frisch decoded the language of the dance.

Von Frisch learned that the direction of the scout's waggling dance tells the workers which way to go. If the scout runs straight up the comb, it means fly toward the sun. If the scout runs straight down, it means fly away from the sun. If the scout runs at an angle across the comb, this indicates the angle the other workers should fly in relation to the sun.

The speed of the dance tells the workers how far to fly. A slow dance, with many waggles, means the food is far away. A fast dance, with fewer waggles, means it is close by. The smell of the flower, which the scout passes to the other workers in a drop of nectar, tells them what scent to look out for.

Returning from a collecting trip, worker bees do a dance on the honeycomb. Any bee that has information about new food sources can indicate the direction, the distance, and even the size of the find by means of this dance.

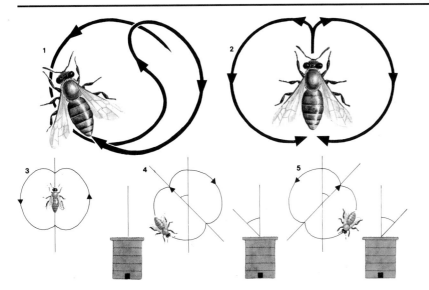

A scout bee can perform two different dances. One called the round dance (1) is used when the source of food is very close to the hive. The more complicated waggle dance (2) gives directions to flowers that are farther away. The straight line of the dance tells the bees in what direction they should fly from the hive (3-5). The number of waggles made by the dancing bee indicates the distance to the food source.

How Did the Code Come into Being?

This communication system enables bees to be very efficient. Each morning, scouts fan out across the countryside, looking for new patches of flowers that have come into bloom. They keep track of where they are by looking at the sun or the patterns of polarized light in the sky. When they find food, they make a beeline back to the hive to get a team of workers to gather the food. The scouts use the dance to tell the other workers where to go.

Nobody knows exactly how this system started. At first, perhaps, a scout might have actually taken the other workers to the food. The scout would come back to the hive, get others excited about the find, and lead them to the flowers. Perhaps a scout turned back after takeoff to gather more recruits. The direction of its takeoff flight would simply point the other workers toward the food. Eventually, the scouts might only pretend to take off—indicating the proper direction without actually leaving the hive. This could be the origin of the waggling run. Other bees would follow the run and know which way to go.

The most difficult thing to explain is how the bees came to do the dance inside the hive. We really have no idea how this happened. But the dance certainly works. In fact, a computerized "robot bee" can do the waggling dance and send worker bees anywhere the computer programmer wants them to go.

4 / Navigating in the Air: Butterflies and Bats

Birds are not the only animals that travel through the air. Baby spiders drift off on parachutes of silk, grasshoppers swarm in search of food, and some butterflies travel long distances in search of shelter.

The most famous migrating butterfly is the monarch. Monarch butterflies live in North and Central America. In autumn, monarchs in Canada begin to fly south in large swarms. Many travel between 1,200 and 1,800 miles (2,000 and 3,000 km) to reach their destinations in Texas, California, and Mexico. There, they hang on trees in huge numbers until spring, when they will head north again, laying eggs as they go.

Butterflies use the sun as a signpost. But, unlike birds and bees, they do not have a built-in clock to tell them whether it is morning or evening. Butterflies traveling north or south will fly toward the sun in the morning. This takes them too far east of their destination. But as the sun moves overhead, the butterflies will adjust their course to follow it. By the evening, the butterflies will be flying too far to the west. The course of migrating butterflies is a

A huge mass of monarch butterflies near its winter quarters in Mexico. These famous migrants will settle on selected trees and stay there during the winter months. When spring comes, the group will fly back north again.

Fruit bats in northern Queensland, Australia. During the daylight hours, the bats hang from trees in large clusters. At night, they visit fruit trees in swarms.

The black flying fox, here hanging on a banana tree, is the largest of the Australian fruit bats. These animals are found in tropical Australia and in Papua New Guinea.

series of loops to the east and the west. The loops cancel one another out, however, so the butterflies actually move in the direction they need to go.

Migrating Bats

Bats are another group of flying migrants. Many bats make special journeys from the roost they use in summer to a different place more suitable for hibernating in winter. In Britain the journeys are short, not much more than 12 miles (20 km). But in North America, some bats spend the winter in caves in Kentucky and then fly 300 miles (500 km) north for the summer. Some Russian pipistrelle bats travel more than 600 miles (1,000 km) to hibernate.

In Australia and the Pacific islands, large fruit bats (also called flying foxes) fly off each evening at dusk to trees that have ripe fruit. The distance may be 12 miles (20 km) or more. When they have eaten all the fruit from the trees, the bats fly off to find more. Some species of fruit bat also make long migrations each year to places that are good for breeding.

5 / Navigating on Land

In Greek mythology, Theseus was a hero who set off to slay the Minotaur, a monster who lived in the middle of a complicated labyrinth, or maze. Everyone who had previously entered the labyrinth had become lost. But a woman named Ariadne gave Theseus a silken thread, which he tied to the entrance of the maze. Theseus killed the Minotaur and followed the thread to find his way out.

Limpets are great navigators. Each limpet in this group has been marked with paint for a scientific experiment. The limpets wander about freely at high tide, but each one will return to its original resting spot as the tide recedes.

Some spiders use the same tactic. Whenever they leave the safety of their hiding place, they spin a silken thread that leads them back to their web. When danger threatens, the spider can climb back along the thread to safety.

Limpets, flattened snails that live on rocks by the seashore, do the same sort of thing. At high tide, the limpet wanders out, feeding on algae that grow on the rocks. But the limpet always returns to the same resting spot before the tide goes back out. To be able to find this spot, the limpet leaves a chemical trail as it travels. The trail points the way back home. Each limpet knows the scent of its own trail. If you scrub a rock clean while the limpets are feeding, you will wipe away the secretions, and the limpets will all become lost.

Ant Navigators

Ants lay trails too. The ants' trails are made of chemical secretions that guide their nestmates to food and help them all get back home.

Following a chemical trail is not really navigation, because, without the trail, the animal would be quite lost. But ants are also capable of real navigation. Some ants navigate by remembering the pattern of plants they saw during their journeys. Other ants use polarized light in the same way bees do.

Some ants use the sun as a compass. If you guide ants along a twig and then turn the twig around, they may become confused because the sun is giving them one message and their trail of secretions is saying the opposite. If you place a mirror next to a line of ants and reflect the sun, the ants may all turn around and head in the opposite direction.

A harvester ant nest in West Africa

A migrating herd of caribou in northern Canada

The Migrating Herds

One of the most dramatic migrations over land is the annual journey of the animal herds that live on the Serengeti Plain in East Africa. In December, at the end of the dry season, vast herds of wildebeests, Thomson's gazelles, and zebras move out of the scrubby woodlands around the edge of Lake Victoria and onto the grassy plain of the Serengeti. The migrating animals go wherever rain is falling, in search of plentiful food. The herds will move toward storm clouds and thunder, even when these are over 60 miles (100 km) away.

Although their exact route varies from year to year, the animals generally travel around the plain in a counterclockwise pattern. By June, when the rains have stopped, the herds move back to the woodlands, which are wetter and provide food even when the plains are dry and dusty.

Other creatures in the Serengeti do not migrate. Lions, for example, stay in one area and feed on the wildebeests when they come through the plain. Giraffes and impalas do not migrate either, but they give birth when the great migration is occurring. With so many animals passing through the Serengeti, there is less chance of a young impala or giraffe being attacked by a **predator** like a cheetah, hyena, or lion.

Opposite: Migrating wildebeests plunge across the Mara River, swimming, if necessary, to keep up with the others.

Above: Wildebeests and zebra cross the Mara River on their migration through Tanzania.

Left: A herd of zebra migrates through Kenya.

6 / *Navigating under Water*

Traveling through water is difficult because an animal may not be able to see the sun or stars and because water currents can sweep an animal off course. Despite that, many creatures do make long, accurate journeys through the water.

Spiny lobsters spend the summer on the coral reefs of the Caribbean islands. As winter approaches, they start to head for deep water. They form a line, each lobster touching the one in front, and begin to walk deeper and deeper. This takes them far below winter storms and out of reach of many predators. It may also cut down on the lobsters' need for food. Deep water is cold. When lobsters are cold, they need less energy and need less to eat.

Spiny lobsters are found around California and the Caribbean Sea. These five lobsters keep close together as they march toward deeper, safer waters.

Fish migrate too. Some fish simply swim from the reef where they live to nearby swamps in order to **spawn** (lay eggs). Others go on long, circular journeys. Some cod travel from Iceland to Greenland and back again. Herring journey around the North Sea. But perhaps the most famous migrating fish is the salmon.

This salmon ladder near Loch More, Caithness, Scotland, helps the migrating salmon climb upstream to get to their breeding grounds.

From Ocean to River

Salmon breed in shallow streams. The newly hatched fish, called **fry**, swim downstream toward the sea. They swim in from many streams and rivers and join others on their journey to the ocean. After several years spent at sea, an adult salmon returns to breed in the very same stream where it was born.

Nobody is exactly sure how a salmon finds its way from the open ocean back to the very river that brought it to the sea. Once there, though, the fish may smell or taste its way home, following chemicals that give each stream its distinct character. The urge to swim upstream is strong; salmon expend great energy leaping up waterfalls and rapids. When people build dams or **weirs**, they often add a salmon ladder, a bypass that enables the fish to continue their journey upstream.

Leaping salmon climb the rapids in a Scottish river.

27

From River to Ocean

Eels make the reverse journey. They are born at sea and travel to fresh water to live there as adults. European and North American eels lay their eggs in the Sargasso Sea in the Atlantic Ocean. The fry drift with the ocean currents until they get close to land. Then they change into young eels called **elvers**, which swim up rivers and become adult eels. The adults live and feed in freshwater ponds and lakes. When they are mature, they retrace their journey to the Sargasso Sea to breed.

The Biggest Navigators

Whales, the biggest creatures in the world, also make long migrations. Many species of whale feed during the summer in icy polar waters and migrate to tropical regions to give birth in the winter months. Gray whales, for instance, swim from Alaska past California to Mexico. If they delay leaving the polar regions as winter approaches, they may get trapped in the ice.

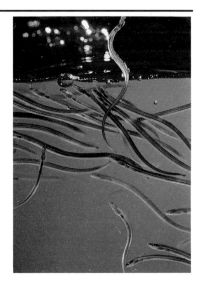

Elvers migrate upstream in Britain.

Several gray whales became trapped in the ice at Barrow, Alaska, in October 1988. They were eventually freed with human assistance.

7 / *People and Navigation*

Some scientists say that people, like pigeons, whales, and bees, have a built-in magnetic compass. In some experiments, people with magnets affixed to their heads weren't able to find their direction as well as people without magnets. The scientists argued that the magnets interfered with the built-in compass in the human brain. Other scientists repeated this experiment and found different results. They say we have no built-in compass, and the argument goes on. Regardless of who is correct, people are still every bit as good at finding their way around as the most skilled animal navigators.

Throughout history, people have found their way without written maps. The Australian Aborigines are still famous for their long journeys. The Aborigines use skills handed down from their ancestors to make their way through the Australian bush. Often, old experienced guides will show younger people the routes through the wilderness and will teach them the secrets of survival. The Aborigines use many different clues to tell them where they are: the position of the sun and stars, the colors of rock, the position of clouds, different types of plants, animal tracks, river beds, and even termite mounds.

The first people to live in Australia were the Aborigines. Like the old man here, the Aborigines knew how to find their way around and how to survive in the bush. They knew about plants and animals and where to find water.

With these signposts, they are able to build a map in their minds.

The most famous human navigators were the Polynesian people of the South Sea islands. The islanders used to make long journeys across the vast Pacific Ocean in small boats. Very often their target was a tiny island that was easy to miss. But the islanders almost always found it.

The navigator was a very important and respected person in the South Sea island community. He apprenticed for a long time with an expert sailor. He learned the star clusters, or constellations, and used their position in the sky to guide the way to different island groups. He would lie on his back in the bottom of the boat and feel the pattern of waves in the ocean. He learned to detect changes in the color of the water, the behavior of fish and birds, and the position of clouds. All this information would give the navigator clues to his location.

Eventually the young navigator was ready to guide his own crew on great journeys across thousands of miles of water. The ancient Polynesian sailors covered a huge area, from Hawaii in the north to Easter Island in the southeast and New Zealand in the southwest. The old ways have been dying out in Polynesia, but young people are again taking pride in the sailing skills of their ancestors. Now there are races around the Pacific to see who is the best navigator.

Outrigger sailing near the Caroline Islands in the southern Pacific Ocean. These young sailing enthusiasts use the same skills and the same kind of boats that their ancestors used.

Glossary

elver: a young eel

fry: a young fish

hibernate: to pass the cold winter months, when food is scarce, in a sleeping or inactive state

instinct: behavior that is inherited rather than learned

polarized light: light waves that have a simple, orderly arrangement and create patterns that can be seen by some insects

predator: any animal that hunts and eats other animals. Lions are predators.

radar: a system of sending out radio waves, which will bounce off an object and return, enabling the radar operator to determine the object's size and location

scout: a worker bee that searches for food and returns to the hive to tell other bees where the food can be found

spawn: To lay eggs

species: A group of animals or plants that have many of the same characteristics and are able to breed with one another

tundra: a cold, treeless plain in an arctic region

weir: a fence or enclosure set in a waterway

Index

Pages shown in *italic* type include pictures of the animals.

This edition first published 1991 by Lerner Publications
Company
Text © Jollands Editions 1991
Artwork © Cassell Publishers Limited 1991

Library of Congress Cataloging-in-Publication Data

Cherfas, Jeremy.
    Animal navigators / Jeremy Cherfas.
        p.   cm.—(How animals behave)
    Includes index.
    Summary: Describes the different ways in which
animals find their way from place to place for migration,
to find food or shelter, or to move around in their territory.
    ISBN 0-8225-2250-0
    1. Animal navigation—Juvenile literature. [1. Animal
navigation. 2. Animals—habits and behavior.] I. Title.
II. Series. III. Series: Cherfas, Jeremy. How animals
behave.
QL782.C47   1991
591.51—dc20   90-13313
                                                         CIP
                                                          AC

Acknowledgments
The publishers wish to thank the following photographers and agencies whose photographs appear in this
book. The photographs are credited by page number and
position on the page (B-bottom, T-top, L-left, R-right):

    Ardea London Ltd.: Jack Bailey, 7B, Dr. C.H.
McDougal, 8; A. Greensmith, 9T; S. Roberts, 9B; John
Mason, 17B; Jean-Paul Ferrero, 21T; Hans and Judy
Beste, 21B; Francois Gohier, 28B. Bruce Coleman Ltd.:
Gordon Langsbury, 3T, 14; Jeff Foott, 4T, 7T; Jane
Burton, 6B, 28T; Frans Lanting, 11; Kim Taylor, 17T;
Peter Ward, 23T; Peter Davey, 24B; J. Pearson, 25; Robert
Schroeder, 26; Nicholas Devore, 30. Eric and David
Hosking: 3B, 10T, 15T. Frank Lane Picture Agency:
W. Wisniewski, 5; W. Broadhurst, 12; Treat Davidson,
18; Ron Austing, 20T; Frank Lane, 20B, 24T; R.
Thompson, 27B. Nature Photographers Ltd.: Hugh
Miles, 4B, 15B, 23B; M. Muller & H. Wolhmuth, 6T;
N.A. Callow, 16; Andrew Cleave, 22; Paul Sterry, 27T.
ZEFA: 13 (both), 29.

Front cover photograph: © Gerry Ellis/Ellis Wildlife
Collection

Editorial planning by Jollands Editions
Designed by Alison Anholt-White
Color origination by Golden Cup Printing Co., Hong Kong
Printed in Great Britain by Eagle Colourbooks Ltd.

Bound in the United States of America